CORRUGATED IRON BUILDINGS

Nick Thomson

SHIRE PUBLICATIONS

Published in Great Britain in 2011 by Shire Publications Ltd, Midland House, West Way, Botley, Oxford OX2 0PH, United Kingdom.

44-02 23rd Street, Suite 219, Long Island City, NY 11101, USA.

E-mail: shire@shirebooks.co.uk   www.shirebooks.co.uk

© 2011 Nick Thomson.

A CIP catalogue record for this book is available from the British Library.

Shire Library no. 592.   ISBN-13: 978 0 74780 783 4

Nick Thomson has asserted his right under the Copyright, Designs and Patents Act, 1988, to be identified as the author of this book.

Designed by Tony Truscott Designs, Sussex, UK and typeset in Perpetua and Gill Sans.
Printed in China through Worldprint Ltd.

11 12 13 14 15   10 9 8 7 6 5 4 3 2 1

COVER IMAGE
The Church of the Ascension, Bedmond, Hertfordshire.

TITLE PAGE IMAGE
The Church of England chapel in the Somerset village of Alhampton, built in 1892, is still in use and is well kept.

CONTENTS PAGE IMAGE
3-inch-pitch corrugated sheet with screw fixing and diamond washer, from St Barbara's Church at Deepcut, Surrey.

ACKNOWLEDGEMENTS
Illustrations are acknowledged as follows:

Abbots Langley Local History Society photo archive, page 22 (bottom); Courtesy of Avoncroft Museum of Historic Buildings, page 24 (both); Jan Baldwin, photographer, page 19; Beamish Museum, Regional Research Centre, pages 29 and 40 (bottom); Anne-Marie Daniel, page 12; Courtesy of Highland Folk Museum, page 28 (bottom); Imperial War Museum, pages 53 and 54; Ironbridge Gorge Museum Trust, pages 27, 38 and 49 (top); Mary Johnson, page 45; Fr D. J. MacKay, St Columba's Cathedral, Oban, page 30 (both); Silvia Mirleman, pages 44–5 (all); Mitchell Library, Glasgow, pages 9, 10 (bottom) and 12 (top); Museum of English Rural Life, pages 16 (bottom right), 17, 23 (top), 33 (bottom), 20 and 48; National Archives, pages 5 (top), 40 (top) and 49 (bottom); Courtesy of the National Trust, page 32 (top); National Trust of Australia (Victoria), page 14; Emma Nicholson, pages 6, 11 (top) and 13; Professor B. Robinson, by kind permission, pages 52 (both); SCRAN, Royal Commission on the Ancient and Historical Monuments of Scotland, page 32 (bottom); Malcolm Seal, page 46 (top); University Library, University of St Andrews, page 56; West Sussex Record Office (doc ref WSRO, Add MSS 2780), page 14; Woodhall Spa Cottage Museum, page 43 (top).

All other photographs are by the author and Caroline Dear.

Shire Publications is supporting the Woodland Trust, the UK's leading woodland conservation charity, by funding the dedication of trees.

CONTENTS

INTRODUCTION

SCATTERED across the countryside, hidden down dead-end village lanes or tucked away on anonymous housing estates are some colourful and quirky little buildings covered in brightly painted corrugated iron. These are the remnants of an industry that thrived in the nineteenth century. Sometimes they appear to be nothing more than rusty eyesores, cheap and tacky temporary expedients that served until a proper building could be put up, but many of these chapels, halls and cottages are older than any of their neighbours.

Corrugated iron buildings are an undervalued part of the heritage of the built environment. They brought character, charm and a lively sense of modernity. Painted in red or green or pink, they introduced new building techniques and innovative forms, with curved roofs and wide spans. Formerly a cutting-edge building component, corrugated iron has become a naturalised part of the rural landscape and an important material for the vernacular builder.

St Philip's Church at Hassall Green in Cheshire was manufactured by Isaac Dixon of Liverpool. Originally located in the centre of Alsager, it is believed to have been moved to its present site by horse and cart in 1883.

4

Such buildings satisfied many of the needs of a changing society. Those that remain express the social aspirations of a bygone era, whether it was for a village hall, a cottage for an emigrant or a church for a new congregation. They were sent out by sea to follow the global trail of colonial expansion, and today they are as likely to be found in South Africa as in Surrey.

Where did these slightly odd, novel and brash buildings come from? Why did they appear, who made them and how old are they? This history of corrugated iron buildings addresses these questions. It will confine itself to the British manufacturers of small-scale buildings. From an early stage, corrugated iron was used for larger structures such as the roof of Paddington station in London (opened in 1854) and the slipways at Pembroke and Chatham dockyards (constructed 1845–7), but the industry in prefabricated corrugated iron buildings was largely defined by the supply of modest-sized kit buildings. There were manufacturers in other countries, too, early examples being M. M. Carpentier & Cie in France and Peter Naylor in New York, but the British manufacturers, being part of the powerhouse of imperial industrialisation, had unrivalled access to worldwide markets.

Whether on a Highland hillside or the African veldt, these pioneering prefabricated structures tell a small part of the history of building construction and there remains a surprising affection for the last of the 'tin tabernacles'.

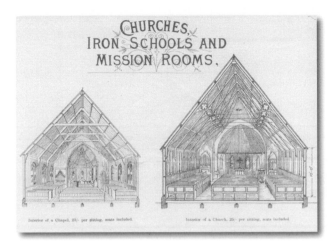

Above: Sectional perspective of a chapel and church from an advertising poster produced by Humphreys Ltd in 1893. The chapel is priced at 23 shillings a sitting and the church at 25 shillings a sitting.

Right: The garrison church of St Barbara at Deepcut in Surrey, built in 1901, is the centre of worship for the Royal Logistic Corps. The British Army regularly used temporary iron churches and at least three were built at Aldershot between 1855 and 1856.

NEW PROPERTIES

A new property is given to Sheet Iron by its being Corrugated, or formed, by powerful Machinery. (Richard Walker's advertisement, 1839)

VICTORIAN ENTHUSIASM for the qualities of iron, and the increasing technical skill in its manufacture, reached a high point in the middle of the nineteenth century. By the time of the Great Exhibition, held in the Crystal Palace in Hyde Park, London, in 1851, it was the material of the age. Not only could it be cast, wrought or formed into thin panels, but the process for making it in corrugated sheets had been known for over twenty years. The exhibition featured a wide range of iron construction products, including corrugated and galvanised roofing, rainwater goods and examples of complete buildings. Prince Albert, the president of the Royal Commission organising the event, would have been able to inspect the work of pioneering companies such as Morewood & Rogers, one of the first entrepreneurs in corrugated iron, Tupper & Carr and Edward T. Bellhouse of the Eagle Foundry in Manchester. Bellhouse had exported cottages and warehouses to California during the 1849 gold rush, and he showed a model of an iron cottage for emigrants, complete with cast-iron columns and corrugated iron walls.

The idea of corrugating sheets of iron and using them as a system to roof over large spans was first patented by Henry Robinson Palmer in June 1829. Palmer was an inventive engineer who had worked with Thomas Telford, and was engaged on the construction of a new basin for the London Docks, which was to include all necessary sheds and warehouses. He wrote in his patent that 'The advantage to be derived from the form or forms proposed consists in the additional strength obtained in the metal itself, so that less aid is required from framework supporting or attached thereto.' It seems that the patent was quickly sold to Richard Walker, a carpenter and builder, also contracted to work on the docks, and it was his firm that first advertised itself as 'Manufacturers of the Patent Corrugated Iron' in *Robson's London Directory* of 1832. His advertisement emphasised:

Opposite:
Loren House, manufactured by John Walker of London and shipped to Australia in 1854. It was originally put up on Curzon Street in North Melbourne and is now at Old Gippstown museum.

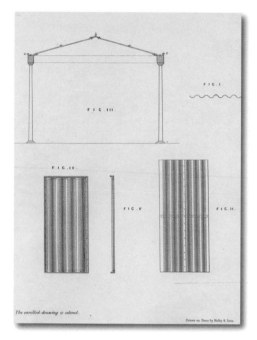

The enrolled drawing is colored.

Drawn on Stone by Malby & Sons.

Illustration from patent number 5786 filed on 30 June 1829 by Henry Robinson Palmer, for the 'Application of Corrugated Metallic Plates to Building Purposes'.

It is particularly recommended for Portable Buildings for Exportation. The small space occupied by stowing them, when the respective parts are separated, rendering their conveyance cheap and easy. For New Settlements, the facility with which they may be erected, or removed from place to place, is a desideratum of great consideration.

The earliest manufacturing process required either fluted rollers or a heavy press that stamped out the corrugations one at a time. This was slow and cumbersome, and the work could easily be spoilt by carelessness in registering the sheets, so that only a few could be produced in a day. Moreover, although the iron sheets were finished with tar or oil paint, they were subject to corrosion. The solution was to coat each side with a thin layer of zinc. The process of galvanising was developed and perfected over a period of five years in Paris by Stanislaw Sorel and brought to England by Commander H. V. Craufurd RN, who took out a patent in 1837.

The benefits of a strong, durable and lightweight material were now evident, and a number of industrialists took an interest in developing corrugated iron buildings. In 1843, John Porter of Southwark, who had sent his son to Paris to study galvanising, constructed the first roof in Britain of corrugated and galvanised sheets. In 1844, John Spencer, an agent for the Phoenix Iron Works of West Bromwich, devised a process for producing corrugated sheets between grooved rollers that was twice as efficient as that previously used, and the early pioneers of prefabricated construction began to explore the possibilities of an export trade in iron buildings.

One of the first to be exported was an iron palace that was sent to west Africa in 1843 for King Eyambo, a prince of the Calabar River on the Gulf of Guinea coast. According to the *Liverpool Times*, this technological wonder, 'built of plates and panels of iron upon a wooden skeleton merely, by Mr William Laycock, iron merchant, of Oldhall Street, was on Friday opened to public exhibition (for the benefit of the charities)'.

The novelty of this new form of building aroused public excitement. The Glasgow firm of Robertson & Lister held a ball in one of their corrugated iron warehouses in 1853, prior to packing it and shipping it to Melbourne. It was viewed with 'delight and astonishment, with external crowds and lines

Laycock's iron palace for King Eyambo, illustrated in *The Builder* in May 1843, was a two-storey building some 50 feet wide by 30 feet deep.

of civic force guarding the living avenues of approach to the scene of the most gay and gorgeous festivities' (*M'Phun's Australian News*, May 1853).

At the Great Exhibition, Prince Albert was impressed by the technical ingenuity and practicality of Bellhouse's iron cottage for emigrants. On one of his morning visits, it was suggested that the Prince might order such a building as an additional room for the Royal Family's new Highland retreat, then under construction at Balmoral in Aberdeenshire. Bellhouse prepared a quote of £194 10s 0d on 4 July 1851, for an 'iron edifice 60 feet long by 24 feet wide, a shell composed of corrugated iron sheets No. 18 Wire Gauge laid upon a framework of iron, including a wooden foundation frame'. By 19 August the completed building was ready for inspection in Manchester, and the whole had been dispatched by train to Aberdeen and erected on site at Balmoral in time for the gillies' ball on 1 October. It served initially as a ballroom, private theatre and dining room before becoming an artist's studio. In 1856 it was relocated near to the stables and game larder, and was converted for use as the carpenters' workshop for the estate. The quality of the iron and the thickness of the sheets have enabled it to survive as one of the oldest remaining corrugated iron buildings still in use anywhere.

Bellhouse, who had developed his prefabricated structures for the Californian gold rush, also became active in the export trade to Australia. An entire theatre seating three hundred people was manufactured by his Eagle Foundry for dispatch to Melbourne. Known as Coppins Royal Olympic Theatre, it was erected in less than six weeks in 1855. However, it was the construction of houses for settlers, particularly in the gold rush towns of Victoria, which occupied most of their attention. One of their cottages, built

The corrugated iron former ballroom at Balmoral, the Royal Family's Highland residence, now in use as a carpenters' workshop.

'Messrs E. T. Bellhouse of the Eagle Foundry, Hunt Street, Manchester, have just finished and are about to send to the Highlands a spacious structure of corrugated iron plates, by command of His Royal Highness Prince Albert' (*Illustrated London News*, 1851).

on the same principles as the Balmoral ballroom, was erected at 42 Moor Street, Fitzroy, South Melbourne, in 1853. It has since been relocated and forms part of the collection of portable iron houses preserved by the National Trust of Australia at Coventry Street, South Melbourne, site of the original 'canvas town' on Emerald Hill in the early 1850s.

Tupper & Carr was another company to benefit from their exposure at the Great Exhibition, progressing from the manufacture of components to that of complete buildings. By 1858 the firm, now known as Tupper & Company, had completed several churches and had been commissioned to build the Presbyterian church at Shrubland Road, Dalston, in east London, at a cost of approximately £1,200. This simple rectangular structure with its narrow pointed windows and stumpy spire was both practical and versatile. It has been reclad in corrugated fibre cement and has changed hands from the

The Patterson House, still on its original site at 399 Coventry Street, South Melbourne. It was one of a group of iron houses imported into Australia from Britain by private speculator Robert Patterson from 1853.

Presbyterians to the Congregationalists and then to the Sight of Eternal Life Church, but it remains a landmark in this part of Hackney.

The supply of prefabricated church buildings was to become a mainstay of the corrugated iron building industry, and one of the pioneers in this field was Samuel Hemming. Initially, his intention was to provide a lightweight and portable house for a son who was about to emigrate. However, his designs were so successful that in 1852 he took over the Clift House Works in Bristol, which he later moved to Bow in London. In the early 1850s

Shrubland Road church in Dalston, London, was built in ten weeks by Tupper & Company in 1858.

One of Hemming's iron churches destined for Melbourne in 1853. Designed to seat nearly seven hundred people, it was intended to provide the many people flocking to the gold diggings with facilities for public worship.

Hemming sent six churches to Australia, and in 1855 he erected the first iron church in London – St Paul's, Kensington. Four years later he sent a substantial church to Victoria in British Columbia. This building could hold a congregation of six hundred, big enough for the chaplain of the Hudson's Bay Company to minister to the spiritual needs of the prospectors drawn to the Fraser River gold rush. Hemming also sent the so-called Moody-Gosset House, a dwelling that remains as an example of his distinctive and economical style. It was shipped from London by the Chief Justice of British Columbia, Matthew Begbie, to Colonel Richard Moody, commander of the detachment of Royal Engineers in the colony, who was appointed Lieutenant Governor and Commissioner of Land and Works there. The following year it was sold to Captain William Gosset, the first Colonial Treasurer.

However, it was the continuing trade to Australia that provided the biggest expansion in the market for corrugated iron buildings. The gold

The Moody-Gosset House, manufactured by Hemming in 1859. It was originally located in Superior Street, Victoria, British Columbia, and has since been moved to Heritage Acres by the Saanich Historical Artifacts Society.

diggings at Ballarat brought an influx of people and a shortage of housing. In 1853 some 6,369 packages of prefabricated iron houses, worth £111,380, were exported to Victoria, and the following year this had risen to 30,329 packages, valued at £247,165. Many of these came from established firms such as John Walker (son of the original patentee), Morewood & Rogers and Samuel Hemming, but these were soon joined by other entrepreneurs. One of the busiest was C. D. Young; originally an ironmonger from Edinburgh, he seems to have taken over the interests of Robertson & Lister in Glasgow and developed a substantial manufacturing capability in casting and corrugating iron, employing over a thousand workmen at his firm's peak, before its bankruptcy in 1858.

A correspondent in the *Glasgow Herald* of 28 March 1853 drew attention to the growth in the export trade:

> More iron houses for Australia – the construction of iron houses to be shipped for Australia is becoming a regular branch of trade in Glasgow. We were favoured on Thursday with the inspection of one of two houses ordered by Messrs Scouller and Walker, fleshers in this city, who are about to leave this country to commence business in Melbourne, and have prudently provided themselves with portable shops and dwelling houses to be used upon their arrival. The difficulty in getting a house built in the metropolis of the gold colony and the expense and loss of time consequent upon such an undertaking are thus obviated; for the structures they have obtained can be put together in a couple of days without trouble.

Corio Villa, a structure combining cast-iron panels and corrugated iron sheets, was manufactured by C. D. Young of Edinburgh in 1854. It was dispatched to Melbourne, but the purchaser died before it arrived, and the packing cases of unidentified parts stood on the quayside until a local merchant acquired them and solved the puzzle of putting them together.

FREDK BRABY & CO., LIMITED

ENGINEERS & CONTRACTORS.

BRABY & CO GALVANIZED IRON & ZINC WORKS

MORE THAN JUST A
COTTAGE INDUSTRY

I beg to acknowledge the largely increasing support with which I have been favoured during the past year and to solicit a still larger share of the patronage of my present and very numerous Customers. (Isaac Dixon's catalogue, September 1874)

THROUGH the second half of the nineteenth century a number of major iron manufacturing and fabricating companies developed in the industrial cities of Liverpool, Manchester, Birmingham and Glasgow, as well as London, which had been the original centre of the corrugated iron industry. Competition increased and Kelly's *Building Trades Directory* of 1886 lists twenty-four firms supplying prefabricated corrugated iron buildings. Each company advertised the special qualities of its products and printed increasingly detailed catalogues to show the wide range of buildings they manufactured.

Producing an economical and long-lasting material was critical to the success of the industry. This depended on the quality and thickness of the iron, and the care with which it was coated in zinc. The thickness of the sheet was measured by the Birmingham Wire Gauge, which generally ranged from the sturdy BWG 16 (0.065 inches, or 1.65 mm) to the lighter BWG 22 (0.028 inches, or 0.71 mm). Thinner sheets of BWG 24 or 26 were manufactured for export to the colonies. The sheets had to be well cleaned and galvanised by hot dipping in a bath of pure spelter, as the raw zinc was called.

The 1874 catalogue of the Liverpool manufacturer Isaac Dixon made a particular point of emphasising the quality of their materials:

Upwards of thirty years' use of this material for roofing and other purposes has fully demonstrated the durability of Galvanised Iron, if made of superior iron and thoroughly galvanised with pure materials. Galvanised iron of inferior quality, i.e. either made from common sheet iron or improperly

Opposite:
Title page of Frederick Braby's catalogue issued in July 1873, showing the offices and works in Euston Road, London.

Cambridge Hall,
Kilburn, London
was originally built
as St James's
Episcopalian
Church in 1863.

Below: Peaton
Church at
Garelochhead in
Argyll was built
in 1870 and
opened for four
months every
summer to provide
holidaymakers with
a place of worship.
Possibly the work
of Isaac Dixon,
it fell into disuse
in 1991.

Below right:
Cover of Isaac
Dixon's catalogue,
published in
Liverpool in
September 1874.

galvanised, has been found, after a few years' use, to entirely disappoint the expectation of purchasers, by showing signs of decay; but this material, when properly prepared and galvanised, forms a permanently efficient roof. In the process of manufacture, even when the very best brands of sheet iron or spelter are used, a small percentage of blemished or imperfect sheets show themselves. In I.D.'s works every sheet, after manufacture, is thoroughly examined, and any such sheets that may be found are thrown aside as *defective*, or waste sheets, and sold as such; so that customers may rely that the whole of the galvanised metal supplied is of a quality to form a thoroughly durable and permanently efficient roof.

This catalogue advertised Dixon's Iron Church, Chapel, School, Dwelling-House and General Iron Building Department, and was directed 'to the

attention of Noblemen, Landed Proprietors, Land Agents, Railway Contractors, Shippers and others'.

Manufacturers were also conscious that corrugated iron buildings might be seen as utilitarian and unattractive, and were keen to promote their aesthetic acceptability. Another Liverpool firm, Francis Morton & Company, had during the mid-1860s established a special department for the manufacture of iron churches, under the direction of the company's own architect. Their catalogue of 1873 contains an extract from *The Illustrated Guide of British Manufacturing*:

> This company has lately turned its special attention to the improvement and development of Iron Church and Chapel building, being anxious to show that this material, in practical and tasteful hands, may be utilized in producing structures at once economical, as comfortable as stone buildings, pleasing in their architectural appearance, and meeting a great desideratum for additional church accommodation throughout the country.

Illustration showing a range of products from the church building department, from Francis Morton's catalogue number 9A of 1879.

They referred to 'close upon 70 churches, chapels and school houses, built by them in various parts of the United Kingdom' by 1879. One of these was

CHURCH BUILDING DEPARTMENT.

The distinguished success which has attended F. M. & Co.'s introduction of an altogether improved system of Iron Church Building is now evidenced by the fact that

THEY CAN REFER TO CLOSE UPON SEVENTY CHURCHES, CHAPELS, AND SCHOOL HOUSES,

Built by them in various parts of the United Kingdom,

REPRESENTING A VALUE EXCEEDING £44,000.

Selections from which are described in F. M. & Co.'s "Illustrated Church Treatise," which will be forwarded on application.

" So desirable a system should be extensively adopted when Home Mission operations are commenced in new districts."—Vide Weekly Review.

F. M. & CO.'S CHURCH BUILDING DEPARTMENT

Is under the superintendence of a qualified Architect specially appointed

for the purpose, and resident at

NAYLOR STREET IRONWORKS.

Illustration of Iron Church built by F. M. & Co. at Kilcreggan.

Illustration of Iron Church built by F. M. & Co. at Blundellsands.

Illustration of Iron Church and Schools built by F. M. & Co. at Northampton.

Illustration of Iron Church built by F. M. & Co. at Birkenhead, Battersea, Forest Hill, Norwood, and Tranmere.

Illustration of Iron Church built by F. M. & Co. at Leeds and Ossot.

St Mark's at Claughton, Birkenhead, opened on 25 April 1867, to seat five hundred people at a cost of £2,000. According to the *Liverpool Daily Courier*, it 'possesses all the beauty, comfort and solidity of a stone church inside, and the outside presents a very pleasing appearance, and strikes one at once as being a substantial and durable structure'.

Frederick Braby & Company was another of the major manufacturing firms to emerge in the second half of the nineteenth century with interests in prefabricated corrugated iron buildings. Braby himself was a clerk who rose through the ranks of the company of Charles Jack to take over the firm in 1854. The company was based in Euston Road, London, but, with Braby in charge, opened new works at Deptford in 1866, acquired docks and then opened a branch in Liverpool in 1871. However, it was their Glasgow works, opened in 1875, which was to be their biggest, eventually covering 35 acres and employing 1,700 people. It continued well into the twentieth century and did not close down until the 1960s. The business directory *Glasgow of Today* in 1888 described Braby's Eclipse Iron and Galvanizing Works at Petershill Road, Springburn, as one of the most notable centres of manufacturing activity in the metal trades of the district:

> The construction of iron buildings and roofings, galvanizing and the manufacture of a wide range of goods in iron, zinc, tin and lead is carried out at the Eclipse Works. Iron buildings go from those works at Barnhill to every quarter of the globe – used for habitation, public meeting, warehousing, manufacturing, and Divine worship. In the colonies, particularly where labour is scarce and costly, one of the first necessities of the settler is a place of habitation and to this requirement the iron buildings produced at and supplied by such establishments as Messrs Braby lend themselves in the most convenient and effective manner. That the advantages of the system of iron buildings thus developed are well recognized is shown by the great progress made in this branch of trade in recent years.

One of the markets that Frederick Braby & Company specifically targeted was in South Africa. In 1871 diamonds were discovered at the farm of the De Beer brothers at Colesberg Kopje. Within a few days, a settlement of tents appeared at New Rush, soon to be replaced by buildings of corrugated iron. Many of these were ordered from the catalogues of companies such as Braby, who advertised as an 'Iron house and church builder' in the *General Directory of South Africa* – 'List of Manufacturers of English Goods for Export to South Africa' – in 1888 and again in 1890. The first church at Kimberley, as the diamond town was now called, was the German Lutheran Church of St Martini. It was built in 1875 from a prefabricated corrugated iron and timber kit and, like much of the rest of the town, it had been brought

850 km overland from Port Elizabeth. After the diamond rush came a gold rush, when corrugated iron was also the first choice of building material. In 1886 Ferreira's Camp was a settlement of four hundred inhabitants and twenty-four iron buildings in the gold district of Witwatersrand. In August that year work started on a corrugated iron hospital and government building at the permanent settlement that had become Johannesburg, and by the beginning of the twentieth century nearly half of the dwellings on the Witwatersrand were of timber and corrugated iron construction.

All the buildings were transported slowly and expensively from the coast. In 1887, a self-made impresario and composer called Luscombe Searelle embarked on the arduous journey from Durban. Travelling first by train, then by ox wagon and coach over the mountain passes of the Drakensberg Range, he brought with him an opera company complete with temperamental singers, costumes, scenery and props. He also brought a corrugated iron theatre. The Theatre Royal was a single-storey building of wood and iron that became known as Searelle's Shanty. Although he quickly sold up, the theatre did illustrate how versatile and ubiquitous the material had become.

There was also an increasing degree of sophistication in the technology of construction and the practical issues of comfort. 'In Iron Buildings there has been a great want of perfect ventilation' says a catalogue issued in 1873. 'Frederick Braby & Company have carefully studied and adopted a complete method, highly approved of by Medical Inspectors of the greatest authority, and used by the Company in their improved construction.' Braby, like other manufacturers at this time, constructed his prefabricated buildings on a timber frame, lined internally with match-boarding. The roof structure was generally of purlins spanning between exposed principal trusses, and again timber-lined on the inside. In tropical climates the corrugated iron cladding could get very hot, and indeed the buildings were sometimes referred to as 'iron pots', so a double-skin system was developed with an air space between the inner and outer leaf, often protected by a layer of inodorous felt, and ventilated at the ridge. Isaac Dixon's catalogue could then claim that 'In Iron Church, Chapel and House Building, I have introduced several very important improvements to meet the requirements of various climates, which make my Iron Erections quite as comfortable as Stone or Brick Buildings'.

The Lutheran Church of St Martini at Kimberley, South Africa, was consecrated in 1875 and remained in use until 1963. It is now at the Big Hole Museum, which celebrates the lives of the diamond miners whom it served.

GALVANIZED IRON HOUSES.

Iron Houses, as constructed by A. & J. Main & Co., are as healthy, comfortable, and convenient as ordinary structures. Special attention is devoted to ventilation and to sanitary and domestic requirements, as well as to the neat and effective finish of the different apartments and fittings. The windows are made to open and close at pleasure, as in ordinary houses; and the apartments are Floored, Lined, and Ceiled with Wood, and finished with Wood Cornices, more or less ornamental according to the character of the house.

Stores and Presses are provided for domestic wants suitable to the size of the house; and sanitary accommodation is always carefully considered. These and other special features secure for A. & J. Main & Co.'s Iron Houses an efficiency and completeness not possessed by any others manufactured.

GALVANIZED IRON COTTAGES.

No. 371.   No. 404.

Ground Plan, No. 400.   Ground Plan, No. 401.

Nos. 371 and 404 are simple and inexpensive arrangements, suitable for Labourers' Cottages, Coolie-huts, &c., singly, or in a range of two or more together.

The Framing is of Wood, with the Roof and Walls of Corrugated Galvanized Iron, floored, lined, and ceiled throughout with Timber. The Roof may be curved or ridge-shaped, the expense being nearly alike.

Referring to the "Ground Plans" it will be seen that Lobby, Store, Presses, Coal-House, and other necessary accommodation are provided for each house. Each apartment is finished with neat Cornices, and Ventilator to open or close at pleasure.

The following are an indication of the

Ground Plan, No. 402.

PRICES.

House of Single Apartment, 14 feet long by 12 feet wide, Door, Windows, &c., with Outhouses, as per ground plan No. 400, in sets of two or more, £47 10s. each.

House of Two Apartments, 24 feet long by 12 feet wide, with Outhouses, as per ground plan No. 401, in sets of two or more, £70 each.

House of Three Apartments, 30 feet long by 18 feet wide, as per ground plan No. 402, £112 10s. each.

All delivered free to nearest Railway Station, or Sea-ports in Ireland.

Only Brick, Stone, or Concrete Foundations require to be provided by purchaser; and the Erection can be done by any Joiner; but, when required, A. & J. Main & Co. send careful workmen, upon very moderate terms, to undertake the complete erection, including concrete foundations, but not the plumber work for water or gas arrangements.

Stoves for Heating or Cooking, with necessary Chimney Piping, not included, but supplied at lowest prices when required.

☞ Estimates given for any other size of House preferred, and Plans and Prices for Cottages of any size, suitable for Gamekeepers, Gardeners, Emigrants, &c., &c., forwarded on receiving dimensions and other particulars.

In transmitting Orders by letter, please quote numbers attached to Design and Ground Plan, and give dimensions preferred.

BUILDING FOR A
CHANGING SOCIETY

Catalogue containing Plans to suit varied requirements, posted free on application. (*The Country Gentleman's Catalogue*, 1894)

IN THE VICTORIAN PERIOD increasing emphasis was placed on the moral and social importance of church-going. At the beginning of the nineteenth century there were around ten thousand parish churches in England. By 1831 the population had almost doubled, and the number of churches had increased by 439. However, over the next forty years this number rose sharply, with 3,204 new churches constructed and 925 completely rebuilt. Here was an ideal opportunity for companies making corrugated iron buildings. The provision of a new church might be undertaken by a philanthropic landowner, a company concerned for the moral wellbeing of its workers or a local committee set up for the purpose. The Church Building Act passed in 1818 allowed for the government to contribute money to match local fund-raising, and by 1868 the Incorporated Church Building Society had helped to finance over a million church sittings, of which 850,000 were free places. In some parishes, particularly in the expanding industrial areas, a single church might be trying to serve the needs of a population of five thousand people or more. Furthermore, the religious revival of the middle of the century and the rise of nonconformism added to the pressure to provide more accommodation. By 1860, Methodists made up 13 per cent of all church membership, Congregationalists 7 per cent, Baptists 5 per cent and Roman Catholics 28 per cent. All these denominations provided a healthy market for the purveyors of ready-made church buildings.

Many of the new churches, chapels and mission rooms were in rural villages or expanding industrial areas on the edge of existing towns. Typical was the Church of the Ascension at Bedmond near Abbots Langley, Hertfordshire. It was built on a spare plot of ground at a crossroads on the edge of the village, donated by the landowner. The church building itself, with its simple bell tower and gothicised windows, was believed to have been surplus to requirements for an export order. It was purchased by Mrs Solly,

Opposite: Corrugated iron cottages advertised in the catalogue of A. & J. Main & Company of Clydesdale Ironworks, Possilpark, Glasgow, January 1882. Prices started at £47 10s for a semi-detached single apartment house, rising to £70 for a two-room version and £112 10s for three rooms.

The match-boarded interior of the Church of the Ascension at Bedmond, Hertfordshire, built in 1880.

the wife of the squire of Bedmond, for £80 and presented to the village in 1880.

Many other churches were built by courtesy of landowners or the local gentry. At Dalswinton in Dumfries and Galloway the Barony Kirk was put up by Mrs McAlpine-Leny of Dalswinton House. She had previously attended the local church at Kirkton and had donated an organ to be played at services there. However, when the organ was unceremoniously removed, she was so incensed that she determined to have her own church. The corrugated iron structure was purchased from the catalogue of Isaac Dixon for the sum of £415 and erected close to Dalswinton House in 1881. Having installed a new minister, Mrs McAlpine-Leny had the satisfaction of playing her organ at the first service.

The Church of the Ascension, Bedmond, photographed in 1908.

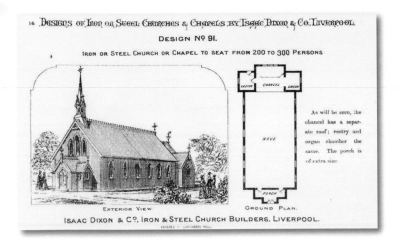

14 DESIGNS OF IRON OR STEEL CHURCHES & CHAPELS BY ISAAC DIXON & Co. LIVERPOOL

DESIGN Nº 91.

IRON OR STEEL CHURCH OR CHAPEL TO SEAT FROM 200 TO 300 PERSONS

As will be seen, the chancel has a separate roof; vestry and organ chamber the same. The porch is of extra size.

EXTERIOR VIEW   GROUND PLAN.

ISAAC DIXON & Cº, IRON & STEEL CHURCH BUILDERS, LIVERPOOL.

Design number 91 from Isaac Dixon's catalogue of 1896 would have cost £297 to seat two hundred people, with a larger version for three hundred people costing £407.

The iron church of St Fillan at Killin in Perthshire was built by the seventh Marquess of Breadalbane. The Marquess entertained shooting parties on his estate, and his guests from the south wanted a suitable place to worship on a Sunday. He ordered a kit building to serve as an Episcopal church, which was built in 1876. The well-heeled visitors had the satisfaction of attending their own familiar services in what the locals came to call the 'Grouse Chapel'.

The Barony Kirk at Dalswinton, Dumfries and Galloway, manufactured by Isaac Dixon in 1881.

Bringsty Common
Mission Church,
Herefordshire,
was manufactured
in 1891 by
Humphreys Ltd.
After the church
was closed, it was
re-erected at
Avoncroft Museum
of Historic
Buildings and re-
dedicated in 1996.

Providing a new church or chapel brought together the enthusiasm of the public-spirited and the zeal of the faithful. At Bringsty Common in the parish of Whitbourne in Herefordshire, the scattered rural community was able to put up a prefabricated mission church. It was a four-bay, timber-lined building, bought from Humphreys Ltd of London in 1891, and served until 1988. Likewise, the people of Westhouses in Derbyshire formed a committee

The interior of
Bringsty Common
Mission Church,
with exposed
scissor trusses
supporting a dark-
stained timber
ceiling, and timber-
lined walls.

St Saviour's Church, Westhouses, Derbyshire, built in 1898 and re-erected at the Midland Railway in Butterley.

and arranged for a church to be constructed. Westhouses was a new settlement built around a locomotive depot in the 1890s. The vicar of nearby Blackwell, Ernest Morris, took a lead in the organisation, which raised £350 by subscription and negotiated a lease for the land from the Duke of Devonshire at a nominal rent. In April 1898 a contract for the building was let, and by September that year the Church of St Saviour was open.

St Fillan's Episcopal Church at Killin in Stirling, the so-called 'Grouse Chapel', was built by the seventh Marquess of Breadalbane in 1876.

The owners of Strines (Calico) Printworks, near Marple in Cheshire, built St Paul's Church in 1880.

Church and chapel buildings were also provided by some paternalistic or socially aware companies, especially where it was thought the application of religious values might lessen the effects of strong drink and rowdy behaviour. St Paul's at Strines, near Manchester, was built by the local calico print works in 1880, while Bailbrook mission church, on a hillside above Bath, was built in 1892 for the workers at Robertson's orchards in an effort to influence their reportedly wild lifestyle of drinking and gambling. These churches were constructed to serve a shifting population swollen by itinerant workers who had no other access to formal worship and spiritual guidance, in an age when this was considered to be good for them. St Chad's mission church was built for the benefit of coal miners at the Granville Mine near Telford, while the mission church at Knowle in Shropshire was a kit, provided by the company and put up by the miners and quarrymen themselves, employed by the Clee Hill Granite Company.

During the course of the nineteenth century, not only did church attendance in general rise, but there was a great increase in the number of denominations. Nonconformist churches grew rapidly in the new industrial society, where the established church did not always address the concerns of the people. Methodism was an important movement, and although Primitive Methodists seceded from the Wesleyan Methodists in 1807 this did not weaken the popularity of Methodism, and its chapels sprang up in many villages and urban slums. In Kent, between 1818 and 1901, some 214

Wesleyan Methodist chapels were constructed, 178 new Baptist chapels and fifty-four Primitive Methodist church buildings. Another stronghold was the Durham coalfield, where pit villages grew up around the new mines, often in isolated areas, in the 1870s and 1880s. In 1990 a survey found that of sixty-five remaining corrugated iron buildings there, fifteen were churches built by the Methodists, two by Baptists, one by Congregationalists and one by Plymouth Brethren.

The mission church in the Shropshire village of Knowle was put up by local quarrymen in the 1880s.

St Chad's Mission Church was built to serve a mining community near Telford in Shropshire in 1888. The prefabricated building is believed to have come from London at a cost of £120. It is now at Blists Hill Victorian Town, Ironbridge Gorge Museum.

This tiny Methodist chapel in the village of Linwood in Lincolnshire is now disused.

In Scotland the story of the Church is complicated by a series of splits and unions that provided ample opportunities for flexible and demountable prefabricated buildings. At the Disruption in 1843 the Free Church left the Church of Scotland, taking with it a third of the ministers. Although the Free Presbyterian Church split from the Free Church in 1893, a union with the United Presbyterian Church in 1900 led to the establishment of the United Free Church. In some areas of the Highlands, however, the congregations voted to remain outside the new unified church, continuing under the name of the Free Church. As a result, in many parishes there was a shortage of church accommodation, and between 1908 and 1914 the Glasgow firm of Speirs & Company manufactured seventy-five buildings for the new United Free Church. The building at Syre in Sutherland is an example of how a congregation might change its allegiance. It was erected in 1891 as a Free Church mission to serve the scattered community of shepherds and

Leanach Church from Culloden near Inverness, now at the Highland Folk Museum, Newtonmore. It was manufactured by Speirs of Glasgow around 1900 and was one of many United Free churches put up at this time.

The Church of Scotland church in the remote township of Syre in Sutherland, built in 1891, may be one of the few surviving examples of church buildings manufactured by Frederick Braby & Company in Glasgow.

gillies in the heart of the Sutherland hills. It may well have been produced by Frederick Braby in Glasgow, judging by the detail of the ridge, which matches their catalogue of 1893. At the turn of the century the congregation voted to join with the United Free Church, and it finally became Church of Scotland when the two churches merged in 1929.

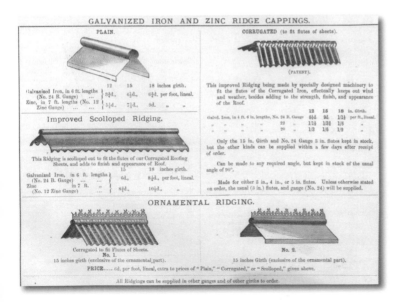

Plain and ornamental ridge details from Frederick Braby's catalogue number 12, August 1893. The church at Syre has pattern number 2, priced at 6d per foot.

The first Roman Catholic cathedral built in Oban was a prefabricated corrugated iron structure erected in 1886.

The interior of the cathedral at Oban.

Corrugated iron prefabricated kits suited the wide range of requirements for religious accommodation. Isaac Dixon's 1896 catalogue shows various designs that could be extended by adding extra bays; for example, design number 81 is priced at £138 to seat one hundred persons, up to £392 to seat four hundred persons. This flexibility in size meant that substantial church buildings, seating over six hundred people, were possible. In Oban, the first Roman Catholic cathedral was a corrugated iron building, constructed thanks to the generosity of the third Marquess of Bute. The Marquess, an enthusiast for the daily observance of high mass, provided the lavishly furnished and decorated pro-cathedral, which served from 1886 for nearly fifty years until the effects of Atlantic gales got the better of it. When the new cathedral was opened in 1934, sheets of the corrugated iron were still being used to board up the gable, until the money could be raised to complete the work.

There was also a growing demand for prefabricated buildings as hospital accommodation. Corrugated iron had been used by the engineer Isambard Kingdom Brunel for some of the buildings in the hospital he designed for the British Army at Renkioi, in Turkey. These were auxiliary buildings with large-span curved roofs, providing facilities such as kitchens capable of cooking for up to a thousand soldiers who had been wounded during the war in the Crimea. The following year, C. D. Young & Company illustrated a military field hospital in their catalogue of 1856, but it was the end of the century before corrugated iron isolation hospitals and temporary wards became commonplace in Britain.

Diphtheria and scarlet fever were endemic in the Victorian period, and before the Second World War patients diagnosed with contagious illnesses would be taken away in a yellow van to the infectious diseases hospital, where they would remain, if they survived, for at least six weeks. One of the most widespread and dreaded diseases was tuberculosis (TB), which was responsible for around a quarter of the deaths in Europe in the nineteenth century. Although the organism that causes TB was identified in 1882, it was not until penicillin came into general use in the 1940s that an effective treatment was available. Local health boards had been in existence since 1848, and hospitals had generally been run by boards of guardians, until that responsibility was taken over by local authorities in 1929. By the 1930s some 32,600 beds were being provided in TB sanatoria in England and Wales.

One of the companies specialising in providing hospitals was Humphreys of London, who built them throughout Britain. One of the few that has survived is Wareham Isolation Hospital in Dorset. It was built in the first years of the twentieth century on a plot of uninhabited heathland outside the town, with two wards, ancillary rooms and a cottage for the nurse. Although it was described as a smallpox isolation hospital, it would have dealt with any infectious diseases until it was closed in the 1960s.

Corrugated iron isolation hospital built by Humphreys Ltd outside Wareham in Dorset in the early 1900s. It has been restored by the National Trust and is available to rent as holiday accommodation.

Speirs & Company
advertised
regularly in
publications such
as the *Northern
Times* at the
beginning of the
twentieth century.

Speirs of Glasgow also constructed many hospital buildings, particularly in the Highlands and Islands. TB was rife in these areas, and speedy isolation of the patient to a small hospital building, often with wards for no more than a couple of people, would have been the best way to avoid the spread of the disease. The report by the County Medical Officer for Argyll, Roger McNeill, in 1905, was a typical story:

Tiree Isolation Hospital – This hospital was only completed at the beginning of the year. It is built of corrugated iron, lined with wood, in accordance with Messrs Speirs and Co's mode of construction for permanent hospitals. The kitchen, with nurse's room, bathroom etc are placed at the centre of the building, with a ward for two beds at each end. An earth closet has been provided for each ward but as they were not found suitable when the hospital was in use, it was decided to have wcs provided.

He goes on to say that on 14 May four cases of diphtheria were notified to him and, taking the first available boat to the island, he found that three children had already succumbed and that two more had sickened. The new isolation hospital was not yet ready to receive patients, but he managed to arrange for furniture and a nurse to be provided, and for the patients to be removed there, and no further spread of the disease was reported.

Among the social changes of the late nineteenth century was the introduction of a formal requirement for schooling, and here too the manufacturers of economical and quickly erected buildings sensed an opportunity. School boards, introduced by the Education Act of 1870, had

Workmen finishing
the construction
of the isolation
hospital at
Baltasound on
Unst in the
Shetlands in 1901.

the power to build and maintain schools out of the rates. Ten years later, the Mundella Act made elementary education compulsory, though still not free nor rigorously enforced, and it was not until 1891 that state education became available for all at no charge.

Isaac Dixon's catalogue of 1896 illustrated ten different school designs. These varied from a simple one-room hall to seat 100–150 children (priced at 3s 10d per superficial foot of ground covered) up to a more elaborate school for 350–550 children (priced at 5s 5d per superficial foot). Dixon's catalogue claims his buildings are well suited for schools as they can be quickly erected and removed at small cost. He says: 'In Colliery, Iron and Manufacturing Districts they are especially useful, as, when a time of great

The former Glenorchy Isolation Hospital at Dalmally in Argyll, built in 1898 by Speirs & Company of Glasgow.

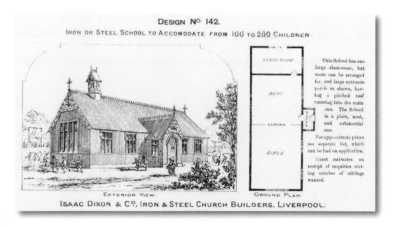

School design number 142 from Isaac Dixon's catalogue of 1896. It was priced at 4s 2d per superficial foot of ground covered.

33

The corrugated iron dining-room and gymnasium at Plockton Primary School in Wester Ross may have been part of the additions to the school made in 1889.

depression in trades comes, and large bodies of workmen leave a particular district, it sometimes happens that schools are closed, without a prospect of their being required again probably for years. In such cases Iron ones can be sold, taken down and put up elsewhere.'

The school boards were keen to build new accommodation. In England and Wales they administered education to over two million children by the end of the century. The leaving age was fixed at eleven in 1893 and raised to twelve in 1899, while in Scotland the nine hundred boards provided

The village hall at Ganllwyd in Gwynedd, originally a mission hall built in the late nineteenth century.

Llanddewi Skirrid village hall, near Abergavenny in Monmouthshire, dates from the early 1880s. It is one of the few such buildings to be listed Grade 2.

schooling up to the age of fourteen, though many still left at the earliest opportunity to earn a wage for the family.

Corrugated iron was also well suited to the provision of village halls. Symbolic of the social cohesion characteristic of many working areas, they were quick and easy for a volunteer committee to buy and put up. Concerts, dances, political meetings, bingo evenings, whist drives and many other community functions have been made possible by these often utilitarian structures. After many decades of service, corrosion and decay set in, and by the end of the twentieth century many halls were being replaced. A few, however, have been successfully renovated. The village hall at Ganllwyd, near Dolgellau in Gwynedd, originated as a nineteenth-century mission hall. Over the years it had deteriorated through rust and damp and was difficult to heat and becoming dilapidated. However, it was completely restored by its owner, the National Trust, and reopened in April 2006, providing a new heart to the village.

The simple but well-maintained village hall at Corgarff in Aberdeenshire. Built in 1895, it continues to serve its community.

Heather Lodge at Kinbrace was built as a shooting lodge in the Sutherland hills towards the end of the nineteenth century.

Another renovated and well-maintained hall is at Llanddewi Skirrid near Abergavenny in Monmouthshire. Originally built as a mission hall for the workmen constructing a nearby reservoir, the hall was moved to its present location in 1885 by a local benefactor for use as a Sunday school and assembly room.

Kit houses, too, were manufactured in corrugated iron and sold in large numbers. One of the principal reasons for the original design of these structures was to provide homes for settlers, which could be shipped around the world, but they also proved attractive to proprietors in Britain as labourers' cottages, shooting lodges and occasionally more substantial dwelling houses. The iron houses advertised in A. & J. Main's catalogue of 1882 ranged in size from a single habitable room, 14 feet long by 12 feet wide, up to a three-apartment unit some 30 feet by 18 feet. Although tiny, they did at least have timber floors and lining, built-in storage and an outside water closet at a time when most workers' cottages would have been extremely rudimentary. 'I am much pleased with the cottage, and my man says he finds it cool and comfortable in the hottest weather,' wrote one customer to Boulton & Paul. The Norwich company advertised its buildings to wealthy landowners who might wish to provide accommodation for gardeners, gamekeepers or labourers, and another testimonial, from Mr J. G. Place of Eriswell Hall, Brandon, Suffolk, added:

> The Portable House supplied by you last year gives entire satisfaction. It was placed in a very exposed position, both to the sun and wind, but at present shows no sign of shrinking at the joints, or the braces giving way. I shall have much pleasure in recommending you to my friends.

Many of the manufacturers advertised shooting lodges, which were becoming popular as a mainstay of the economy in some remoter areas of Britain.

Garlies Lodge at Glentrool near Minnigaff in Galloway was manufactured by Humphreys Ltd in 1910. It was built by the Earl of Galloway to accommodate shooting and fishing guests.

Paying guests could enjoy the splendour of the hills from the comfort of a well-appointed house. Heather Lodge in Sutherland served this purpose, having been delivered by train after the railway to Wick and Thurso had been completed in 1874. Rose Bungalow at Morden in Dorset also started life as a shooting lodge, beside a decoy pond on the Charworth Park Estate. It was dismantled and moved to its current location in 1939, where it was used by the wartime volunteer services, before becoming a private house. At Glentrool, in the south of Scotland, a substantial lodge was built by the Earl of Galloway, who wanted to attract paying guests to his shooting and fishing estate. Garlies Lodge, built in 1910 by Humphreys Ltd, is modelled on their colonial designs, with wide verandah and servants' quarters. It provided comfortable timber-lined living and dining rooms, a modern bathroom and a separate motor house complete with covered porch, garage and rooms for the chauffeur and two maids.

Rose Bungalow at Morden in Dorset was originally used by shooting parties of local gentry.

ROWELL'S IMPROVED GALVANIZED IRON BUILDINGS.

Special Designs and Estimates supplied free on receipt of a rough plan, showing size of building, accommodation required, &c., &

GARDENER'S COTTAGE. No. 117AC.

Size 23 ft. × 20 ft.
Contains 4 Rooms, Pantry, and Offices.
Timber framed and lined with match-boarding.
Price fixed complete, exclusive of foundations, £140.

IRON STABLE. No. 118AC.

Size 17 ft. × 14 ft.
Coach House and 1 Stall.
Price, fixed complete, exclusive of foundations,
floor or fittings .. .. £48.

CRICKET PAVILION. No. 119AC

Size 30 ft. long × 12 ft. wide.
Price, fixed complete. exclusive of foundations £63

CHURCH OR CHAPEL TO SEAT 400 PERSONS.

No. 120AC.

Designs and Estimates supplied free of charge for temporary or permanent Buildings — plain or ornamental, and to suit all purposes.

Our Illustrated Church List, No. 398, free on application.

Neat Church, with Vestry, Chancel, Organ Chamber and Porch. Size over all 70 ft. long by 35 ft. wide, 10 ft. to eaves, 22 ft. to apex. Framed in substantial well seasoned timber, lined with match-boarding and felt, covered with best quality 24 G Galvanized Corrugated Sheets ; Flooring, tongued and grooved ; inside stained and varnished ; outside woodwork painted three coats ; Gutters and Downpipes, Locks, and all ironmongery for complete erection.

Price, delivered to nearest station, and erected on site on purchaser's foundation, **£360 net.**

IRON WAREHOUSE. No. 121AC

Size 20 ft. × 12 ft.
Price, fixed complete, exclusive of foundations, lining or flooring .. .. .. £
Lined and floored, £9 10s. extra.

IRON STORE. No. 122AC.

Size 20ft. × 10 ft.
Price, fixed complete, exclusive of founda-tions, lining or flooring £2
Lined (sides and ends), and floored, £8 extra.

VILLAGE CLUB HOUSE. No. 123AC

Size 30 ft. long × 20 ft. wide.
Price, fixed complete, exclusive of founda-tions .. .. £105.

MISSION HALL. No. 124AC.
TO SEAT ABOUT 150 PERSONS.

Size 35 ft. × 20 ft. with porch 6 ft. square.
To seat about 100.
Price, fixed complete, exclusive of foundations, £130.

INFECTIOUS HOSPITAL. No. 125
FOR 8 BEDS.

Size 40 ft. long × 20 ft. wide, to accommodate 1 with lean-to 10 ft. × 6 ft. Fitted with partition W.C. and Lavatory.
Price, fixed complete, exclusive of foundations .. .. £135.

DAVID ROWELL & CO., 31, OLD QUEEN ST., WESTMINSTER, LONDON, S.W.
Westminster Works : HYTHE RD., WILLESDEN, LONDON, N.W.

Telegrams—
"Rowell, London.
"Minuteness,
London."

BUILDINGS IN STOCK

Buildings dispatched same day as order received. (Humphreys Ltd poster, July 1893)

THE LAST DECADE of the nineteenth century was the period of peak production of corrugated iron buildings. They were not only more plentiful, but also more affordable. A single sheet of Frederick Braby's premium quality 'Sun Brand' (very best, selected sheets and double-coated in pure spelter), with a thickness of 18 BW gauge and 6 feet in length, would have cost 4s 8d in August 1893 and had risen only to 5s 1d by July 1914. Annual production of corrugated iron sheets had reached over 200,000 tons in 1891, of which 150,000 tons was being exported, mostly to the new colonies of the British Empire. By 1900 the total exported had risen to 250,000 tons. The corrugated sheets were also becoming more standardised. Early manufacturers had made sheets in a variety of different profiles, thicknesses, lengths and widths, but by the 1890s the 3-inch pitch (distance from ridge to ridge) was becoming most common. Braby's Catalogue No. 12 (August 1893) advertised: 'sheets with corrugations of 1, 2, 4, and 5 inches can be supplied but only 3 inches corrugations kept in stock.' They also produced what they called 'Canadian Pattern' sheets, with small corrugations 12 inches apart, which are characteristic of some older buildings.

When corrugated iron kit buildings first became readily available in the 1850s they were innovative and promised quick and easy building, but they were not necessarily cheap. Shrubland Road Church, built in 1858 in Dalston, east London, was a modest rectangular building 37 feet wide by 72 feet long, and had cost between £1,200 and £1,300, or well over £2 per sitting. St Mark's in Birkenhead (built 1867) cost £2,000 at £4 per sitting. In the 1870s and 1880s these buildings still cost many hundreds of pounds to purchase (Bishop Auckland Baptist Chapel, 1876, cost £950; St David's at Tudhoe cost £403 18s 0d, still over £2 per sitting) but by the end of the century prices were relatively much cheaper. A small chapel or mission hall for one hundred people could be bought for around £100. This compared to

Opposite:
Advertisement for David Rowell & Company in *The Architect's Compendium and Catalogue*, 1901, showing their buildings, ranging from an iron store for £29, through cricket pavilions at £63, to a church seating four hundred at £360.

Typical church designs by Humphreys Ltd from an advertising poster printed in July 1893.

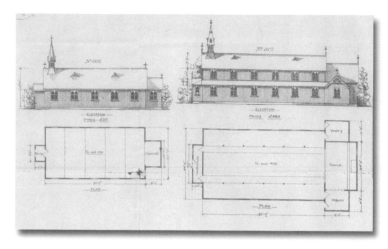

Various grades and profiles of corrugated iron illustrated in Frederick Braby's catalogue printed in September 1939, but never issued because of the outbreak of war.

HIGH-GRADE GALVANIZED CORRUGATED SHEETS.

THE life of a Galvanized Sheet depends upon the coating of zinc or galvanizing. Hence it is real economy to use High-grade Galvanized Sheets.

Our Sheets answer this description and we give the galvanizing of the Sheets our special care. All Sheets are well coated with zinc.

Having our own Rolling Mills and Galvanizing Plant we can regulate the quality from raw material to finished product ; the result is that our Sheets ARE WITHOUT A SUPERIOR ON THE MARKET.

We have the largest variety of corrugations and can produce sheets to suit any requirement.

Lengths, 4' to 12'. **Widths,** 1' to 4'. **Gauges,** 12 to 30 gauge.

Can be supplied Curved to any radius.

THE "BRABY" QUALITY MEANS LONGER LIFE.

Braby's " Sun " Brand—Very Best Double-Coated.

Braby's " Empress " Brand—Extra Heavily Coated.

Braby's " Eclipse " Brand—Extra Coated : Specially Selected.

Braby's " Castle " Brand—Good Ordinary Quality : Prime Sheets.

Braby's " Voxol " Brand—Good Ordinary Quality : Ex Liverpool Stock.

Some of our types of Corrugation.

between £5 and £10 per sitting for a more conventional stone or brick neo-Gothic edifice.

Typical of the intense competition was David Rowell & Company, of Old Queen Street, Westminster, London. Their advertisement in the *Architectural Compendium* of 1901 offered a mission hall to seat 150 people, fixed complete but excluding foundations, for a price of £130, and a full-sized church for £360. They supplied the church of St Barnabas at Caversham, Reading, which opened in June 1898. It cost £410 for the building, with an extra £15 for the foundations and brick base, and £32 17s 7d for the gas fittings and heating stove. The committee also decided on a bell for £6 and a pulpit for £4 10s 10d as essential furnishings for their new building. By the time *Laxton's Price Book* was published in 1912, a number of companies could advertise churches from just 15s a sitting.

In a catalogue of 1896, Isaac Dixon wrote:

We have during the last 10 years erected upwards of 150 Iron Churches on our improved system and in all cases they have been much approved. In all our designs we endeavour to combine economy in cost with a neat and tasteful appearance and the utmost comfort in use.

The Mission Room at Clows Top in Worcestershire was built in 1895. A local subscription raised the £70 18s 0d it cost to purchase the building.

Iron Churches can now be erected at very low prices. One that would cost 35/- per sitting about four years ago can now be put up for about 20/- per sitting. A plain but neat Iron Church or Chapel to accommodate 200 persons can be erected for £240 exclusive of interior fittings, foundations, heating and lighting; these would add about £70; thus making the total cost for a Church for 200 persons exclusive of land, completed ready for Divine Worship about £310 or 30/- per sitting.

Rowell manufactured the first Church of St Barnabas at Caversham, Reading, in 1898 for £410. The building is still in use as the Parish Centre.

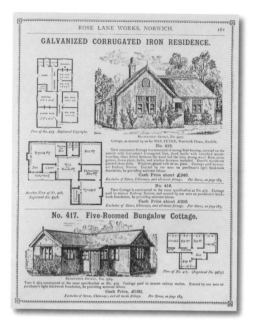

A page from Boulton & Paul's catalogue produced in the 1890s showing a cottage very similar in plan to the building at Woodhall Spa, Lincolnshire.

Cottages, too, were very competitively priced. In 1873 Francis Morton & Company were offering a five-room cottage, erected on site, for the sum of £120, while by 1888 Boulton & Paul's catalogue advertised a similar-sized dwelling for £112, 'Erected by our men on Purchaser's foundation, exclusive of all inside fittings, stove and chimney'. Boulton & Paul were one of the major manufacturers to emerge at this time. Their ironmongery and agricultural supply business, based in Norwich, quickly diversified and they became manufacturers of a full range of prefabricated buildings. Many of their cottages were delivered by rail, such as the house at Woodhall Spa in Lincolnshire which was transported in sections to nearby Kirkstead station in 1884. Three years later, it was relocated nearer to the centre of the fashionable resort town, where it provided a house for Thomas and Mary Wield, who had been employed by the syndicate that ran the spa baths. Thomas made the donkey-drawn Bath chairs that took visitors around the village, and their son, John, later added a photographic studio to the building, which became a museum in 1987.

The maturing industry had an impressive capacity to deliver its products: for example, William Cooper Ltd claimed that a hospital could be dispatched within twenty-four hours and would be erected and ready for occupation within fourteen days. They continued: 'Any Building not in stock, or special sizes, can be placed on rail within a few days from receipt of order.' Likewise, Humphreys Ltd had developed rapidly and by 1893 were publishing sales posters that emphasised their products' assets of durability, stability, simplicity, facility of erection and removal, and fitness for all climates; they boasted of experience of constructing over ten thousand iron buildings in all parts of the world. 'Buildings are in stock', they said, 'at the Grounds and Works, Knightsbridge, Hyde Park, London SW; dispatched same day as order received.'

One market that was opening up to them was in South America. At the end of the nineteenth century the development of Patagonia for extensive cattle farming began in earnest. The harsh climate of the extreme south, with its bitter winters and frequent gales, combined with the lack of any indigenous building materials, meant that prefabricated corrugated iron buildings were ideally suited to the needs of the settlers. Humphreys kept an office in Buenos Aires and regularly shipped out kit buildings both as homes for the emigrants and as farm buildings for the estates.

The cottage at Woodhall Spa in 1888, showing a donkey-drawn Bath chair made by Thomas Wield.

The *estancia* of Guer Aike, shown on pages 44 and 45, was designed with typical north-facing glazed galleries to catch the sun, running between generously sized family rooms. Built by Humphreys in 1915, it even had the comfort of underfloor central heating. It was fully pre-assembled in England, then taken apart, marked for dispatch and shipped, with all the components carefully packed and ready for construction.

William Cooper was also in the export trade, making use of the advice of former residents abroad, and making sure the packing for shipment 'has the greatest attention, so that the parts may be protected from rough usage,

The Boulton & Paul cottage at Woodhall Spa, Lincolnshire. In 1987 it became the Woodhall Spa Cottage Museum.

The Humphreys works in London around 1915, with the building for Guer Aike being assembled prior to dispatch to Argentina.

The Humphreys works. The signs read 'Humphreys Ltd. Country Residences Knightsbridge S.W.' and 'Bungalows for erection in Patagonia no. 32131'.

consequent upon a long voyage and transhipments and carriage overland'. Their specification included a 4-inch-thick timber framework, with a layer of felt to keep out the draughts, and thickly coated corrugated iron cladding. Match-board lining and deal floorboards finished the interior,

while the exterior could be embellished with an 'ornamental finish to gables and pinnacles studied from the most approved Gothic designs'. Cooper built Devan Haye, a two-storey house in Sherborne, Dorset, in 1889, for Mr Dalwood, a local chemist and developer. It was brought from the works in London by train, and taken by cart to the site in the garden of an existing house on the edge of town. The new building, which originally included a two-storey servants' block and stables, had to be sufficiently substantial to satisfy the stipulation that at least £400 be spent on it, and it seems from the catalogue that the kit itself would have cost about £350 erected on purchaser's foundations, or £250 cash price put on rail or wharf. Cooper priced their projects either for erection on site, or for supply only. Erection on purchaser's foundations included the painting of all the outside woodwork in two coats of 'best oil colour' and staining and varnishing the interior timber, plus carriage within 100 miles of London. The 'on-rail' price offered a drawing 'to facilitate erection, supplied with each building' and put on rail at the works or delivered to London Wharf.

The firm also supplied a three-bedroom house built at Dulnain Bridge in the Scottish Highlands in 1915. Notwithstanding the exigencies of the First World War, the Seafield Estate decided they required additional accommodation for their guests during the shooting season. The two-storey timber-lined cottage arrived by train and included such modern conveniences as a bathroom and toilet. In the Lincolnshire village of Little Cawthorpe is a corrugated iron house which is probably also the work of William Cooper. Colonial Cottage, with its hipped roof, wide verandah

The Humphreys building as constructed at Estancia Guer Aike, Argentina.

45

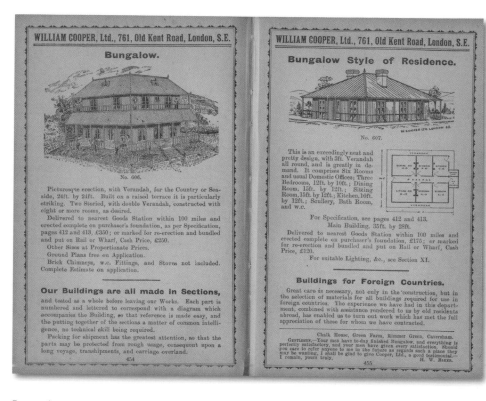

Extract from a catalogue of William Cooper Ltd published in the early twentieth century showing single-storey and two-storey houses.

Devan Haye, a two-storey house with verandah built in Sherborne, Dorset, in 1889 and bought from the catalogue of William Cooper.

Colonial Cottage at Little Cawthorpe in Lincolnshire is probably a William Cooper design, dating from 1910.

and pairs of French windows, is a classic example of the prefabricated bungalow. It appears to have been built in 1910 (judging by the bits of newspaper stuffed in the walls) and closely resembles Cooper's design number 607, which would have cost £175.

Balintomb Cottage at Dulnain Bridge in the Highlands was supplied by William Cooper in 1915.

In the competitive marketplace for corrugated iron buildings, each manufacturer tried to surpass his rivals. William Cooper, like many others, included testimonials elicited from satisfied customers:

Harlington, Hounslow
Dear Sirs, – Mr Sugery wishes me to say that he is very well pleased with
the Iron Building erected by you
Yours Truly
H. C. Belch, Jun. Clerk to the Parish Council

Mr Belch does not go into detail on the nature of the iron building procured.

Some companies also had a standard approach to the requirements of particular building types and may not have been above 'borrowing' designs from the opposition. There are sometimes striking similarities between catalogues. Dixon's church number 107, Cooper's design number 565, the church by Lightfoot & Ireland and Humphrey's church number 40 all have a similar aisled plan, small spire and five bays of Gothic-arched windows – which suggests more than a mere coincidence of aesthetic treatment.

The industry was not, however, entirely unregulated. By the end of the nineteenth century the steady introduction of local government by-laws, based on model by-laws regulating temporary iron buildings produced by

Isaac Dixon's church design number 107, to seat three hundred persons, from their catalogue of 1896, offered for £583.

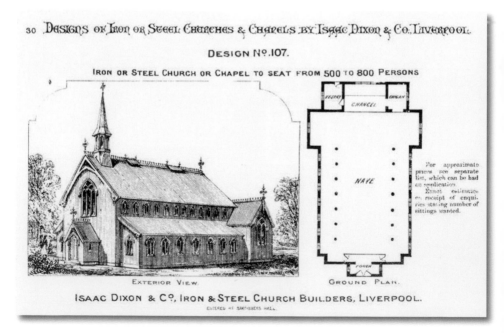

30 Designs of Iron or Steel Churches & Chapels by Isaac Dixon & Co. Liverpool.

DESIGN No.107.

IRON OR STEEL CHURCH OR CHAPEL TO SEAT FROM 500 TO 800 PERSONS

EXTERIOR VIEW.   GROUND PLAN.

ISAAC DIXON & Co. IRON & STEEL CHURCH BUILDERS, LIVERPOOL.

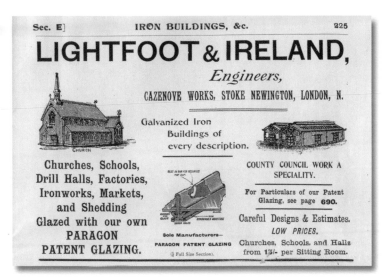

An advertisement
for galvanised iron
buildings of every
description from
Lightfoot & Ireland,
in *The Architect's
Compendium and
Catalogue*, 1901.

the Local Government Board in 1888, was starting to effect a degree of
control. In some ways though, the gathering weight of regulation was
beneficial to the success of corrugated iron. For example, in Iceland after
1903 the building regulations in Reykjavik required that houses be clad in
corrugated iron as a form of fire precaution. This came mostly in sheet form
from Britain and was used to produce a colourful and exuberant 'corrugated
chalet' style of Icelandic architecture.

Illustrated
selection of
Humphreys
churches, with
options for church
fittings, seats,
rostrums and
reading desk.

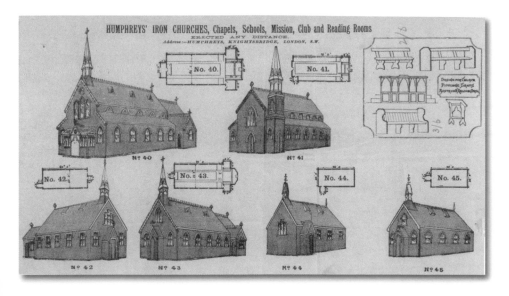

A KINDLY
DOMESTIC BEAST

It has already earned a high character as a useful, tractable, kindly, domestic beast. (Filson Young, writing about the Nissen hut in the *Daily Mail*, 6 February 1917)

The United Free Church in Plockton, Wester Ross, was one of many built by Speirs of Glasgow in the early twentieth century.

IN THE SIX YEARS leading up to the First World War, Speirs of Glasgow built twenty-seven hospitals, fifty-seven schools and seventy-five churches in the Highlands and Islands, and their erection teams worked as far afield as Wales and Ireland. The company first appeared in the Glasgow *Post Office Directory* in 1893 as 'Speirs & Co – iron and steel churches, houses and weatherboard buildings contractor, 125 West Regent Street', and it was this new use of steel that defined the buildings of the twentieth century.

Although still generally referred to as corrugated iron, sheets of profiled cladding could now be made in a stronger metal. Steel is made from pig iron with a carefully controlled carbon content (0.15 per cent for mild steel, up to 1.5 per cent for high carbon steel). Henry Bessemer patented a method of making it in 1855 by blowing air through pig iron in a converter, but it was not until the 1890s that a process for producing thin steel sheets suitable for corrugating was developed. Steel was stronger, but it was more difficult to achieve a good quality of galvanisation, and so it did not catch on immediately. Nonetheless, as early as 1896 Isaac Dixon's company was offering the choice of steel as an option for their churches. They wrote:

> We ask special attention to our newly introduced Galvanised Corrugated Steel for Churches etc ... This is stronger than Iron, is Galvanised with a thicker coating of spelter and possesses numerous advantages over any other metal used. The cost of a Steel Church will be about 4/- per sitting more than an Iron one. It is well worth the difference, and we invite the careful attention of intending purchasers to this material.

At the beginning of the twentieth century the production of prefabricated buildings remained a thriving business. For example, between 1901 and 1902 a complete new settlement with a population of nearly one thousand was built in the Peak District. This was Birchinlee, nicknamed 'Tin Town',

The church at Fort Augustus on the Caledonian Canal, by Speirs & Company.

Birchinlee, built in 1901–2 to house men working on the Howden and Derwent dams in Derbyshire, became known as 'Tin Town'. This street of corrugated iron houses included a greengrocer's shop on the left and a tailor's on the right.

constructed by the Derwent Valley Water Board to house the workmen who were building the Howden and Derwent dams, and their families. These dams were the biggest masonry structures in the country at the time and were needed to supply water to the growing cities of Sheffield, Nottingham, Leicester and Derby. The Act that created the board included a statutory obligation to provide satisfactory accommodation, in contrast to the squalid conditions normally endured by the navvies who worked on the great civil engineering projects of the period. The village was self-contained and built entirely of corrugated iron. There were semi-detached 'huts' for up to ten

An extension being added to the Derwent Canteen at Birchinlee in 1903. The only place in the village licensed to sell alcohol, the canteen partially subsidised other social functions through its profits.

single men, married men's quarters and smaller cottages for each foreman and his family. There were various shops, a public house, a bath-house, a school, a general hospital and an isolation hospital. There was also a recreation hall, where the social life revolved around concerts, dances, hand-cranked film shows and an annual horticultural show for produce grown in the village allotments. The village vanished from the upper Derwent valley as quickly as it had appeared. When the dams were complete, the buildings were dismantled and sold off to new owners. In October 1914 the War Office bought fourteen of the hut blocks and re-erected them as part of a prisoner of war camp at Lofthouse Park in Wakefield.

The provision of temporary hutted accommodation was to exercise the minds of the military during the First World War but it took a leap of imagination by a Canadian mining engineer to provide an ingenious solution – and one of the most ubiquitous forms of prefabricated corrugated iron building. At the beginning of 1916 Peter Nissen was stationed at Ypres with the 103rd Field Company Royal Engineers. Knowing there were insufficient billets for soldiers in the devastated villages round about, he sketched an idea for a cheap mass-produced hut that could be put up quickly by unskilled troops in all terrains.

The first prototype Nissen Bow Hut was ready in May 1916. It had a semicircular lightweight steel frame supporting twenty-eight interchangeable curved corrugated sheets for the roof, and each end was completed with timber gable panels, which came with the windows already fitted. The final model, 16 feet wide by 27 feet long, went into production in August 1916. Two companies, Braby & Company and John Summers & Company, manufactured the corrugated iron sheeting, while Boulton &

Some of the earliest Nissen huts being erected in November 1916 near Bazentin, between Amiens and Arras in France. (Imperial War Museum Q 4597)

53

Colonel Nissen
talking to a
sergeant outside
one of his huts at
Blangy, south-west
of Amiens, in 1917.
(Imperial War
Museum Q1743)

Colonel Nissen talking to a sergeant outside one of his huts at Blangy, south-west of Amiens, in 1917. (Imperial War Museum Q1743)

Paul made the timber panels. There was snow on the ground in northern France by December that year but already twenty thousand huts were providing shelter for the hard-pressed soldiers. The Nissen hut was designed to be assembled from the minimum number of components, none of which would be heavier than could be lifted by two men. The parts were to be packed on a single lorry, leaving room for three men, and the complete building could be put together by a team of six in no more than four hours. By the end of the war Major Nissen had provided 100,000 huts, each accommodating twenty-four men, together with ten thousand larger hospital huts.

Nissen huts continued to be used for many years afterwards in both military and civilian life. Nissen himself formed a manufacturing company and in 1925 designed a prototype mass housing unit with a curved corrugated iron roof. Yeovil Borough Council in Somerset built twenty-four as an experiment but they were not a success, being more expensive than a conventional house.

Nissen huts saw service again in the Second World War, and in 1941 a larger version, the Romney Hut, was introduced, which was 35 feet wide by 96 feet long. The Americans produced a similar building called the Quonset Hut, developed at Quonset Point, Rhode Island, though generally the corrugations ran horizontally along the sides. The original Nissen hut, however, cheap, simple and versatile, continued to be an exemplary model of prefabricated building.

Corrugated iron was the first major industrially produced sheet cladding material. Many manufacturers used it for large-scale projects such as factories

Second World War Romney huts on the island of Tiree in western Scotland. During the war Tiree was an important staging post for RAF flights over the Atlantic.

and railway stations in addition to prefabricated buildings on a domestic scale. However, after the late boom of wartime manufacturing, the flair and inventiveness of the Victorian pioneers gave way to a utilitarian functionality more suited to warehouses and bus garages. In addition, in 1907 the Austrian engineer Ludwig Hatschek invented a machine to manufacture corrugated sheets of asbestos cement, a new wonder material and competitor to corrugated iron.

St John's Church Hall in Meadowfield near Durham, a utilitarian corrugated iron structure built in 1909 by D. Cowieson & Company of Glasgow.

THE UPS AND DOWNS OF IRON SHEETING

BRITISH COMPANIES led the way in designing and manufacturing prefabricated corrugated iron buildings and thereby pioneered a new approach to construction. Their story is one of industrial development and social change. Richard Walker, the original manufacturer of 'Patent Corrugated Iron', first advertised in the *South Australian Record* on 27 November 1837. He drew special attention to his 'Portable Buildings for Exportation' and so commenced a trade in which buildings were manufactured in Britain and supplied around the world.

The development of corrugated iron was a part of the gathering pace of change in the building industry. Portland cement was patented in 1824, the Hoffman continuous brick kiln was invented in 1858 and steel production was made possible in processes developed by Bessemer, and later Siemens, in the 1860s. However, corrugated iron buildings were not universally welcomed, and received, at best, a mixed press. A correspondent writing to *Building News* (15 January 1858) about a church designed by the eminent architect Matthew Digby Wyatt, and manufactured by Tupper & Company, noted: 'Mr Wyatt's Corrugated Iron Church was doubtless a structure of stern necessity for exportation to Rangoon ... how indocile to the Ithuriel touch of an architect is this very untoward material.'

Corrugated iron buildings were nonetheless a great success, the result of advantages in cost and construction time. The companies that arose in the second half of the nineteenth century became major manufacturers, continuing well into the twentieth century. Francis Morton printed the foreword to their catalogue in three languages. Frederick Braby, Isaac Dixon, Humphreys Ltd and others left their trademark labels on thousands of buildings.

By the end of the twentieth century, however, they were becoming scarcer. In Britain, not many more than thirty were categorised as Listed Buildings. Typical is the Church of St Andrew at The Wern, Minera, near Wrexham. It was listed Grade II in 1998 as 'a particularly unaltered example of the corrugated iron mission churches, built in relatively large numbers in

Opposite:
In 1909 St James's Roman Catholic Church in St Andrews, Fife, was sold to Mr J. D. Spence, who had it moved in four sections to be re-erected as a roller-skating rink.

In 1878 Queen Victoria donated a piece of land for a new church and school at West End, Esher, Surrey, to provide for the spiritual needs of the aged, poor and infirm. The following year St George's was opened at a cost of £300.

'Dunstalking' is a brightly painted corrugated iron cottage in the village of Kinbrace in Sutherland.

the period 1890–1914, but now becoming rare'. Even Listing is no guarantee against demolition, though a number of buildings have been saved by relocation to the collections of open-air museums such as Avoncroft Museum of Historic Buildings near Bromsgrove, Worcestershire, and the National

Left: The manufacturer's label of Speirs & Co. on a corrugated iron church at Minard in Argyll, built in 1910.

Below left: Manufacturer's label on a church at Portsonachan in Argyll. It reads: 'F Smith & Co. Iron Buildings Manufacturer, Carpenters Road, Stratford, London E.'

Bottom: The Church of St Andrew at The Wern, Minera, near Wrexham, was built in 1882.

The label of Humphreys Ltd on the window sill at Garlies Lodge in Galloway.

Trust for Australia's Portable Iron Houses museum at Coventry Street, South Melbourne.

Venerable examples of these structures dating from the 1850s still survive, showing that, when well maintained and regularly painted, a corrugated iron building may outlast other forms of construction. The quality and care of the original manufacturers of the late nineteenth and early

Isaac Dixon's label on the side of the Barony Kirk at Dalswinton near Dumfries.

The Barony Kirk at Dalswinton near Dumfries.

twentieth centuries can be seen in the remaining churches, halls and homes that still fulfil the purpose for which they were designed. Though they tend to be undervalued, these jaunty and friendly buildings can continue to add delight and character to our built environment.

Detail of horizontal 5-inch-pitch corrugated iron on the side of the former ballroom, at Balmoral Castle, Aberdeenshire.

FURTHER READING

Dickinson, H. W. 'A Study of Galvanised and Corrugated Sheet Metal',
Transactions of the Newcomen Society (1943), pages 27–35.

Emery, N. 'Corrugated Iron Public Buildings in Co. Durham', *Durham
Archaeological Journal* 6, 1990.

Fladmark, J. M.; Mulvagh, G. Y.; and Evans, B. M. *Tomorrow's Architectural
Heritage, Landscape and Building in the Countryside.* Mainstream
Publishing, 1991.

Herbert, G. *Pioneers of Prefabrication, The British Contribution in the Nineteenth
Century.* Johns Hopkins University Press, 1978.

Irving, R. (editor). *The History and Design of the Australian House.* Oxford
University Press, Melbourne, 1981.

Mornement, A., and Holloway, S. *Corrugated Iron Building on the Frontier.*
Frances Lincoln, 2007.

Morriss, R. K. *The Archaeology of Buildings.* Tempus Publishing, 2000.

Robinson, B. *Memories of Tin Town: The Navvy Village of Birchinlee and Its People.*
J. W. Northend Ltd, 2001.

Smith, I. *Tin Tabernacles, Corrugated Iron Mission Halls, Churches and Chapels of
Britain.* Camrose, 2004.

Thomson, N. and Banfill, P. 'Corrugated Iron Buildings: An Endangered
Resource Within the Built Heritage', *Journal of Architectural Conservation*,
volume 11/1 (2005).

Walker, B. *Corrugated Iron and Other Ferrous Cladding.* Historic Scotland
Technical Advice Note, 2004.

Detail of a Humphreys church at Warren Row in Berkshire. St Paul's Mission Church was built in 1894, and cost £104 14s.

The Church of Scotland church in the village of Tomatin in the Highlands was originally built as a United Free church in 1910.

PLACES TO VISIT

Avoncroft Museum of Historic Buildings, Redditch Road, Stoke Heath, Bromsgrove, Worcestershire B60 4JR. Telephone: 01527 831363. Website: www.avoncroft.org.uk

Blists Hill Victorian Town (Ironbridge Gorge Museum), Legges Way, Madeley, Telford, Shropshire TF7 5UD. Telephone: 01952 88439. Website: www.ironbridge.org.uk

Chiltern Open Air Museum, Newland Park, Gorelands Lane, Chalfont St Giles, Buckinghamshire HP8 4AB. Telephone: 01494 871117. Website: www.coam.org.uk

Highland Folk Museum, Kingussie Road, Newtonmore, Highland PH20 1AY. Telephone: 01540 673551. Website: www.highlandfolk.com

Kent Life, Lock Lane, Sandling, Maidstone, Kent ME14 3AU. Telephone: 01622 763936. Website: www.kentlife.org.uk

The Midland Railway – Butterley, Butterley Station, Ripley, Derbyshire DE5 3QZ. Telephone: 01773 747674. Website: www.midlandrailwaycentre.co.uk

Museum of East Anglian Life, Crowe Street, Stowmarket, Suffolk IP14 1DL. Telephone: 01449 612229. Website: www.eastanglianlife.org.uk

St Fagans: National History Museum, Cardiff CF5 6XB. Telephone: 029 2057 3500. Website: www.museumwales.ac.uk/en/2807

Weald & Downland Open Air Museum, Singleton, Chichester, West Sussex PO18 0EU. Telephone: 01243 811363. Website: www.wealddown.co.uk

Woodhall Spa Cottage Museum, The Bungalow, Iddesleigh Road, Woodhall Spa, Lincolnshire LN10 6SH. Telephone: 01526 353775. Website: www.woodhallspa-museum.co.uk

INDEX